Welcome to the Solar System

D1822885
9781782965688

Our solar system is made up of the Earth and seven planets that orbit the Sun. Other things also orbit the Sun, such as dwarf planets, and rocks called asteroids. In this book you will discover lots of out of this world facts about these planets, their moons, and asteroids!

Saturn

Venus

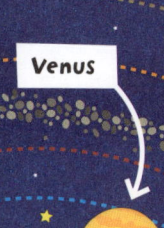

Mars

Uranus

Sun

Earth

Jupiter

Neptune

Mercury

Our solar system (in order)

Inner planets:
Mercury, Venus, Earth, Mars.

Outer planets:
Jupiter, Saturn, Uranus, Neptune.

M   V   E   M   J   S   U   N

The Sun

The Sun is an enormous star at the centre of our solar system. Even though the Sun is 93 million miles away from the Earth, we see the Sun's light and feel the Sun's heat every day.

Stars are giant spheres of burning hot gas that radiate heat and bright light. The gases in the Sun have been burning, rising and cooling over and over again for millions of years.

The temperature of the Sun is 5,500 degrees Celsius. At its centre it is 15 million degrees Celsius!

The Sun's gravity controls the orbit of the planets in our solar system. Gravity is a powerful force that keeps the planets spinning and orbiting in a fixed place, instead of floating away and colliding into each other.

SPACE FACT!

The Sun is so enormous that you can fit 1 million Earths inside it.

Solar Shading

Planets spin as they orbit the Sun, so only one side of a planet faces the Sun at any time. On Earth when it is day, we are facing the Sun, but on the other side of the Earth it will be night. Colour each Earth below to show which side is day, and which is night.

The Sun is responsible for the Earth's climate and weather. Its heat and light creates day and night, and summer and winter on Earth. Even though we are far away from the Sun, its light is so strong that you should never look directly at it.

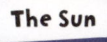

The Sun

Mercury

Mercury is the first planet in our solar system, and is the closest planet to the Sun, at 36 million miles away.

Mercury is also the smallest planet in our solar system. Even Jupiter's and Saturn's moons are bigger!

As it is so close to the Sun, Mercury is very hot. On Earth, a warm day in London usually reaches 26 degrees Celsius. On Mercury, a hot day is usually 430 degrees Celsius!

SPACE FACT!

One day on the planet Mercury lasts as long as 59 Earth days!

Mercury is very rocky and dry, and covered in enormous craters several miles deep! With no weather or atmosphere on Mercury, it is unlikely that life could ever survive there.

Interstellar Puzzle!

Three of these facts are true, and three are false.
Draw a circle around the facts you think are true.

1. Mercury is the 3rd closest planet to the Sun.

2. One day on Mercury lasts 100 Earth days.

3. Mercury is the smallest planet in our solar system.

4. It can reach 430 degrees Celsius on Mercury.

5. There are huge craters on Mercury's surface.

6. There are lots of thunder storms on Mercury.

Mercury

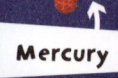

Answer: 1. False, it is the closest. 2. False, one day lasts 59 days. 3. True. 4. True. 5. True. 6. False, there is no atmosphere, so no weather, and no storms.

Venus

SPACE FACT!

Venus is the slowest spinning planet.
One day on Venus lasts 243 Earth days!

Even though Mercury is closest to the Sun,
Venus, the second planet in our solar system,
is the hottest. The temperature on the surface can
reach over 480 degrees Celsius. Venus's atmosphere
is rich in carbon dioxide, which traps heat between
the surface and the clouds, and stops heat escaping.
The 1000 volcanoes on Venus also keep the surface of
the planet hot too. Some volcanoes are even 12 miles across!

Venus spins in the opposite direction to the other planets
in the solar system. This means that
on Venus the Sun rises in the west
and sets in the east.

Venus is the second brightest object
in our night sky, after the Moon.
You can see Venus at sunrise and at
sunset. It is so bright that sometimes
it can even be seen during the day!

Crazy Craters!

The surface of Venus is full of craters. Some are small but some are miles wide. The largest craters have even been given names.
Can you unscramble the names of these craters?
What is the connection between them?

1. DINAL
_____

2. HELOC
_____

3. AENJ
_____

Venus

Answer: 1. Linda. 2. Chloe. 3. Jane. The connection is that the largest craters all have girls' names.

Earth

The Earth is the third planet in our solar system. It was formed approximately 4.54 billion years ago and is the only known planet in our solar system to support life.

The atmosphere and climate on Earth has created the perfect environment for life. The air we breathe is 78% nitrogen, 21% oxygen and 1% other gases. 70% of the Earth's surface is covered in water. Because of this, the Earth looks like a brilliant, shining blue orb when viewed from space.

On 20 July, 1969, the first astronauts landed on the Moon. Neil Armstrong was the first to walk on the Moon, followed by Buzz Aldrin. It took them 3 days to fly there in a spacecraft. They wore special, heavy space suits and took oxygen so they could breathe on their moonwalk.

The ocean tides on Earth are caused by the gravitational pull of the Moon. Gravity has about 17% of the effect on the Moon as it has on Earth. This means that while on Earth you can walk around on the ground, on the Moon, instead of walking you will float!

Moon

SPACE FACT!

The Earth is the only inner planet in our solar system to have a moon.

Walking on the Moon

Draw Neil Armstrong's footsteps on the Moon!

Earth

The Moon

Mars

SPACE FACT!

The biggest volcano in the solar system is on Mars. Olympus Mons is 373 miles wide and 17 miles high!

Travel to Mars could one day be a reality. It would take 7 months to fly there, and you would need to take specially built cabins to live in on the surface, as there is no oxygen on Mars.

Mars is the fourth planet in our solar system. It is called the Red Planet because of the iron minerals that rust in the atmosphere, turning the soil red.

Mars is similar to Earth. One day lasts for 24 hours, it has an elliptical orbit around the Sun, and, because it is tilted like Earth, it has seasons and polar ice caps.

Cosmic Colouring

Use the key to colour in this picture of Mars.
Each colour indicates a different feature of the planet.

1. Blue — Ice Caps
2. Dark Red — Craters
3. Light Red — Surface

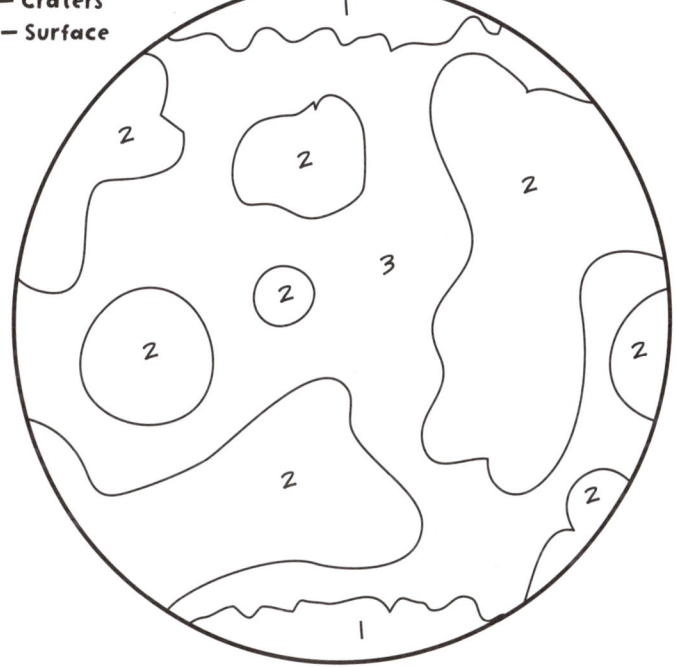

If you visited Mars, you would need to check the weather reports regularly; Martian weather can be extreme! The largest dust storms in the solar system are found on Mars. Some storms are so strong, they cover the entire planet and last for months!

Mars

Jupiter

Jupiter is the fifth planet in the solar system. It is called a gas giant because it is the biggest planet, and it is mostly made of gases. Jupiter is also the fastest spinning planet, with one Jupiter day lasting only 10 Earth hours.

The speed at which Jupiter spins makes its gas clouds form visible bands, creating Jupiter's colourful, stripy appearance.

In one of these gas bands is a large red spot. This 'Great Red Spot' is a huge storm that has been raging on the planet for more than 300 years.

Jupiter has 67 moons. Some of these moons are small, but others are enormous. Ganymede is Jupiter's largest moon, at 10,272 miles wide!

SPACE FACT!

Jupiter is so big that 1000 Earths could fit inside it. You could even fit three Earths inside the Great Red Spot!

Colour and Copy

Four of Jupiter's moons are the most well known. Astronomers are still studying and naming the rest! Use the key below to draw them in, then colour to complete this picture.

Don't forget to colour the Great Red Spot!

Io

Europa

Callisto

Ganymede

Jupiter

Saturn

The sixth planet, Saturn is another gas giant. It is, oddly, the lightest planet in our solar system. If you built a swimming pool large enough, Saturn could float on it! This is because Saturn is mostly made from lighter-than-air hydrogen gas!

Saturn is well known because of its seven rings. These thin rings are actually ice crystals, and only measure 10 metres thick.

Saturn is the second fastest spinning planet, rotating at 6,200 miles per hour. Its fast speed means that it is wider in the middle and flatter at the poles. It also spins at an angle to the Sun, which gives Saturn summer and winter seasons.

On Earth, our summer lasts three to four months, but on Saturn, summer lasts about eight Earth years!

SPACE FACT!

Watch out for lightning strikes on Saturn. In 2004 the 'Dragon Storm' created lightning strikes 1000 times more powerful than the lightning we have on Earth.

Complete the Picture

Can you figure out what is missing and draw it in?
If you get stuck the answer is at the bottom of the page.

 Saturn has over 50 moons, but the largest moon is called Titan. Titan is so big that it is the second biggest moon in the solar system. It is also the only moon in the solar system to have a thick atmosphere and clouds, like a planet.

Saturn .

Answer: Saturn is missing its seven rings!

Uranus

Uranus was the first planet to be discovered by telescope. Uranus's colour is caused by its methane gas atmosphere which filters out red light, making the planet appear blue-green.

Uranus is one of two ice giants in our solar system. Even though it is the seventh planet and still close to the Sun, Uranus is the coldest planet in our solar system. If you visit Uranus, wrap up warm. Its temperature only reaches -216 degrees Celsius!

Uranus is the only planet to spin on its side. Because of this, its rings rotate up and over the planet instead of around its middle.

SPACE FACT!

Astronomers think Uranus spins on its side because of a collision during its formation.

Counting Moons

Count the moons below to discover how many orbit Uranus.

Uranus

Answer: There are 27 moons!

Neptune

At 2.8 billion miles away, the eighth planet, Neptune, is the furthest from the Sun. Like Uranus, Neptune is an ice giant, and it's green–blue colour is due to the methane gas in its atmosphere.

SPACE FACT!

It would take 12 years to fly to Neptune!

It takes Neptune 165 Earth years to orbit the Sun. This means that since its discovery in 1846, Neptune has only orbited the Sun once.

The gravity on Neptune is similar to the gravity on Earth, but you could never stand on Neptune – you would sink straight through the layers of gas.

Triton is one of Neptune's 14 moons. It is the coldest world in our solar system. It spews freezing cold nitrogen out from the ground making the temperature a chilly -235 degrees Celsius!

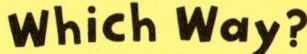

Draw a line through the stars to help the rocket fly to Neptune. Careful not to fly into any stars on the way!

Neptune

Space Exploration

Ever since humans first looked at the stars, we have made many discoveries about the Earth and our solar system. Then space exploration changed forever when, in 1957, the first satellite, called Sputnik flew into space.

Before humans could travel in space, we had to learn how to fly there, and how to survive there. In order to leave the Earth's atmosphere, a spacecraft needs the full power of a rocket to fly into space.

Once in space, astronauts must rely on special spacesuits to provide them with air to breathe, and protection from extreme temperatures. They also need to take plenty of food and water, and fuel for their spacecraft to return home to Earth.

SPACE FACT!

Neil Armstrong's first words on the Moon were:
"That's one small step for a man, one giant leap for mankind."

Design and Draw

Imagine that you are about to travel in space. What would your spacecraft look like? Design and draw your own spacecraft below.

Comets, Shooting Stars and the Asteroid Belt

Planets and moons are not the only things you can find in space. There are other interesting objects, such as comets, meteors, and asteroids.

The tail and fuzzy glow around a comet is called a 'coma'. When the comet nears the Sun, the frozen water and carbon dioxide in the comet change quickly from a solid into a gas.

Comets are made of ice, dust and rocky debris. They get their name from the Greek word meaning 'hair of head' as they were thought to look like stars with hair.

Halley's Comet takes 76 years to orbit the Sun and produces a meteor shower, which can be seen on Earth twice a year as we pass through its debris.

Meteor showers happen when comet debris burns up in Earth's atmosphere.

Meteorites are rocks that are too big to burn up when they hit the Earth's atmosphere. About 38,000 meteorites have been found on Earth. The largest, Hoba, weighed 119,000 pounds (54,000 kg).

Shooting stars aren't actually stars. They are small bits of dust, like grains of sand or pebbles that fall into the Earth's atmosphere. They enter the atmosphere at amazingly fast speeds and burn up creating a bright light, which we can see from the ground.

The asteroid belt is made up of billions, if not trillions, of rocks and debris that orbit together around the Sun. The asteroid belt is situated between Mars and Jupiter.

Jupiter's enormous size and gravitational pull keeps the asteroid belt in one place. Some rocks are the size of a grain of sand, but some are big enough to be called small, or dwarf planets.

Occasionally a large piece of rock, called an asteroid, drifts away from the belt into a planet's orbit. Scientists believe an asteroid once collided with the Earth, causing the extinction of the dinosaurs.

Moon Maze

Can you help the spacecraft fly safely through this asteroid belt maze to land on the moon?

Dwarf Planets

There are four criteria that define a dwarf planet.

Dwarf planets are neither planets or moons!

1. It orbits the Sun, like other planets.

2. It is a round planet shape.

3. It has rocky debris around it.

4. It does not orbit another planet.

Pluto is the second dwarf planet from the Sun. It was classified as the ninth planet until 2006, when it was declassified, as it has not cleared the objects from the area around its orbit.

Haumea is the third dwarf planet from the Sun. It has an elongated shape because it rotates so quickly, causing it to stretch as it spins.

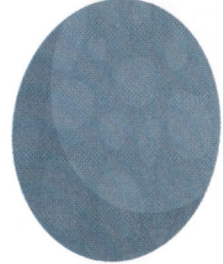

Makemake is the fourth dwarf planet from the Sun, but it is so bright you can see it with a good telescope!

Ceres is the closest dwarf planet to the Sun, as it is located in the asteroid belt. It is the only dwarf planet in the inner solar system. It is the smallest of the known dwarf planets.

Eris is the biggest of the dwarf planets and the furthest from the Sun. You could fit all of the asteroid belt inside Eris. It takes Eris over 550 years to orbit the Sun!